AMAZING WORLD WAR II STORIES

NIGHT WITCHES AT WAR

THE SOVIET WOMEN PILOTS OF WORLD WAR II

by Bruce Berglund
illustrated by Trevor Goring

Consultant:
Tim Solie
Adjunct Professor of History
Minnesota State University, Mankato
Mankato, Minnesota

CAPSTONE PRESS
a capstone imprint

Graphic Library is published by Capstone Press,
1710 Roe Crest Drive, North Mankato, Minnesota 56003
www.capstonepub.com

Library of Congress Cataloging-in-Publication data
Names: Berglund, Bruce R., author. | Goring, Trevor, 1952– illustrator.
Title: Night Witches at war : the Soviet women pilots of World War II / by Bruce Berglund ;
    illustrated by Trevor Goring.
Description: North Mankato : Capstone Press, [2020] | Series: Graphic library amazing
    World War II stories | Audience: Ages: 8–14. | Audience: Grades: 4–6. | Includes
    bibliographical references and index.
Identifiers: LCCN 2019005962 (print) | LCCN 2019014190 (ebook) | ISBN 9781543573190
    (eBook PDF) | ISBN 9781543573152 (library binding) | ISBN 9781543575507 (paperback)
Subjects: LCSH: Soviet Union. Raboche-Krestianskaia Krasnaia Armiia. Voenno-Vozdushnye
    Sily—History—Juvenile literature. | World War, 1939–1945—Aerial operations, Soviet—
    Juvenile literature. | Women air pilots—Soviet Union—History—Juvenile literature. |
    Bomber pilots—Soviet Union—History—Juvenile literature. | Night flying—Soviet Union—
    History—Juvenile literature. | World War, 1939–1945—Women—Soviet Union—Juvenile
    literature.
Classification: LCC D792.S65 (ebook) | LCC D792.S65 B485 2020 (print) |
    DDC 940.54/4947—dc23
LC record available at https://lccn.loc.gov/2019005962

Summary: In graphic novel format, tells the amazing story of the Soviet Night Witches and their
courage while flying nighttime bombing missions on the front lines during World War II.

EDITOR
Aaron J. Sautter

ART DIRECTOR
Nathan Gassman

DESIGNER
Ted Williams

PRODUCTION SPECIALIST
Katy LaVigne

Design Elements by Shutterstock/Guenter Albers

All internet sites appearing in back matter were available and accurate when this book was sent
to press.

Direct quotations appear in **bold italicized text** on the following pages:
Pages 7, 9: from *Wings, Women, and War: Soviet Airwomen in World War II Combat*, by
    Reina Pennington, Lawrence, KS: University Press of Kansas, 2002.
Page 29, panel 2: from "Women Veterans of Aviation in the Soviet Union," by Reina Pennington
    in *A Soldier and a Woman: Sexual Integration in the Military*, edited by Gerard J. DeGroot
    and C.M. Peniston-Bird. New York: Pearson Education, 2000.
Page 29, panel 3: from "Nadezhda Popova, WWII 'Night Witch,' Dies at 91," by Douglas Martin,
    The New York Times, July 14, 2013. https://www.nytimes.com/2013/07/15/world/europe/
    nadezhda-popova-ww-ii-night-witch-dies-at-91.html

Printed and bound in China. 5174

TABLE OF CONTENTS

Nearly two years after World War II (1939–1945) began, Nazi Germany launched the largest military invasion the world had ever seen on June 22, 1941.

More than 3 million soldiers, 3,000 tanks, 7,000 artillery, and 3,000 airplanes crossed the border into the Soviet Union.

Soviet forces were caught by surprise. Thousands of planes were destroyed before they could take off.

The Nazis bombed many Soviet cities and villages. Millions of people died—more than in any other country during World War II.

People across the Soviet Union volunteered to defend their homeland.

Many women and teenage girls joined the army. Others joined their neighbors and used whatever weapons they could find.

Some women became pilots and fought the Nazis from the skies.

German forces soon learned to fear their attacks. The Nazis often called the female pilots the "Night Witches." Their skill and success in battle would make them heroes of the Soviet Union.

JOINING THE SQUADRONS

After the Nazi invasion, hundreds of Soviet women wrote to Marina Raskova. They wanted to serve their country as pilots, and they asked for her help.

Three years before the war, Raskova became famous for being part of a historic flight across the Soviet Union. Her crewmates broke the world record for the longest flight ever made by women.

Lieutenant Raskova, you parachuted from the airplane into the Siberian forest--in a snowstorm! Why did you do this dangerous thing?

We were almost out of fuel. After I jumped, the plane weighed less. My comrades were able to fly further and break the record.

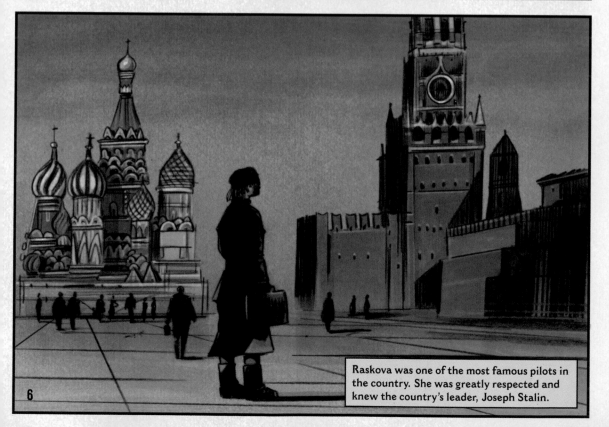

Raskova was one of the most famous pilots in the country. She was greatly respected and knew the country's leader, Joseph Stalin.

It is too dangerous to have women fight as pilots.

People will not forgive us for sacrificing young girls.

These girls are already going to the front lines to fight, Comrade Stalin. They are taking matters into their own hands. Soon, they will even steal airplanes to protect the motherland.

We can't have girls fighting in a war. That's a job for men.

But comrade, these women are trained pilots. We need their help to defend the motherland.

In the end, Stalin agreed with Raskova's arguments. The Soviet military created three squadrons of women pilots. Raskova was named the commander.

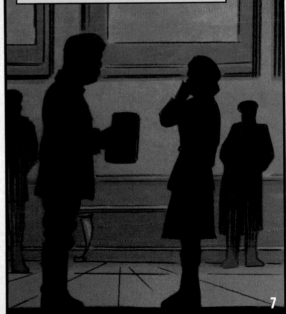

Women came from across the Soviet Union to serve in the air squadrons. The military had no uniforms for women, so they had to wear men's uniforms.

Some of you have left school to be here. Some of you have left your own children behind. All of you have sworn to defend our motherland to the last breath!

Training was difficult. Most of the women had flown small planes before. But now they had to learn to fly fighters and bombers.

The women had several accidents during training. Many of the newer Soviet planes had been destroyed by the Nazis. So the women's squadrons had to train with older, broken-down planes.

Many of the male officers were against women having their own squadrons. But others knew that women could fly as well as men.

I've received 112 little princesses. Just what am I supposed to do with them?

They're not princesses. They're pilots. And they're here to fight, just like the men.

Women did the same jobs that the men did in their squadrons. Each one did her part.

Pilots flew the fighters and bombers into combat.

Navigators studied maps and plotted the course for the planes.

Armorers loaded the planes with bombs and ammunition for battle.

Mechanics made sure the planes worked properly.

BATTLES IN THE SKY

In 1942 the Nazis were at the height of their power. Their empire stretched across Europe.

Europe 1942

The Nazis believed that people in the Soviet Union were worth less than Germans. They ruled over the lands they conquered with terrible cruelty.

Axis-Controlled Territory

Allied Nations

Neutral Nations

Three Soviet women's squadrons were sent to fight on the front lines. They flew three types of planes on different missions.

DADADADADADA

Fighter planes fought to stop the Nazi air force from striking Soviet troops.

Dive bombers were used to keep German troops away from towns and cities.

ZIP! ZIP! PFFT! CHUK!

TRAT-TRAT-TRAT-TRATT

Slow-flying biplanes were often used for sneaky nighttime attacks. They bombed camps of German soldiers and supplies.

ZZZHEEEE ...

KA-BOOM!

The women who flew fighter planes tried to keep German bombers from attacking Soviet cities.

BRZBRZBRZBRZBRZ!

BRZBRZBRZBRZBRZ!

In April 1943, two female fighter pilots encountered a large force of enemy planes.

Commander, I count 42 enemy bombers approaching. I repeat, 42 bombers. What are our orders?

What are your orders? Attack! ATTACK!

The two pilots attacked the German bombers alone.

DADADADADA!

DADADADADA!

They shot down four of the German planes.

KA-PLEW!

We're under attack! It must be a squadron of fighters! Release your bombs and return to base!

Although they were outnumbered, the two Soviet women chased the rest of the bombers away. They saved a railway station and thousands of soldiers from being attacked.

Command, they're turning back. I repeat, the enemy is turning back!

Dive bomber pilots attacked Nazi forces with deadly accuracy.

Target is below. I'm going into our dive.

The pilots steered the plane into a steep dive toward the target.

When the plane was close to the ground, the pilot would release the bombs.

Bombs away!

vvzZVVZZVVZZVVZZVVZ

KA-BOOM!

KA-BOOM!

KA-BOOM!

The Soviet dive bomber attacks were deadly for Germany's forces. Nazi fighter pilots tried to shoot the Soviet planes out of the sky to protect the ground troops.

KA-POW!   KA-POW!

KA-POW!

TAT! TAT! TAT! TAT!

During one mission, the plane flown by Lyuba Gubina was hit by fighters.

We're hit!

TZING!

TZING!

We're going down! We have to bail out!

You go first! We'll find each other on the ground!

THE NIGHT WITCHES

The most famous of the Soviet women's squadrons was the 46th Night Bomber Regiment.

BRZBRZBRZBRZBRZ!

BRZBRZBRZBRZBRZ!

BRZBRZBRZBRZBRZ!

Target is ahead. Attack formation.

They flew under the cover of night to attack German forces behind the front lines.

Hurry! We must have these shells ready for the attack.

As they approached their target, the night bomber pilots would turn off their biplanes' engines.

BRZBRZBRZBRZBRZ ... CLICK

wwwwWHHHHHOOOOOOOSSSSSHHHH!

The only sound from their planes was a whooshing in the dark. It sounded like a flying broomstick.

It's the Night Witches!

BOOM!

BOOM!

BOOM!

Take cover!

There! It's the Night Witches!

KA-POW!

KA-POW!

KA-POW!

The Night Witches flew the Po-2 bomber. It was an old biplane that Soviet pilots had flown for many years. Because the planes were slow, they were easy targets for soldiers on the ground.

Antiaircraft fire was a terrible danger to the Night Witches. The bullets easily ripped through the old planes' canvas coverings.

We're hit!

ZIP!

I have to turn back. Our only chance is to land the plane somewhere.

ZIP!

The planes had to carry as many bombs as possible, so heavy parachute packs were left behind. If a plane was hit by enemy fire, the pilot and navigator could not bail out. Several brave Night Witches went down along with their planes.

SCREEEEE...

SCREEEEE...

SCREEEEE...

We're not going to make it! Prepare to crash!

DANGEROUS MISSIONS

That was our tenth mission tonight. And we have two more before sunrise.

I'm too tired to get out of the cockpit.

The women who flew the night bombers faced many dangers. They dropped bombs on their targets, returned to the base for refueling, and then took off on the next mission.

Here's some hot tea. It'll help you stay awake--and keep warm.

Many pilots and navigators were lost when their planes were shot down. One who survived was Nina Raspopova.

Nina and her navigator were flying in the mountains in southern Russia, in December 1942, when antiaircraft fire hit their plane.

BOOM!

We're hit! The whole bottom of the cockpit has been blown away.

ZIP!

We have to make a crash landing.

Nina managed to land the crippled plane. The navigator was badly wounded, but Nina freed her from the wreckage.

Nina was also injured. Antiaircraft fire had blasted the wooden frame of the airplane. She had large splinters stuck in her body.

Nina, it's too far back to our side of the lines. Go on without me. I'm too badly hurt.

No, I won't leave you. The Nazis will kill you. We can make it together.

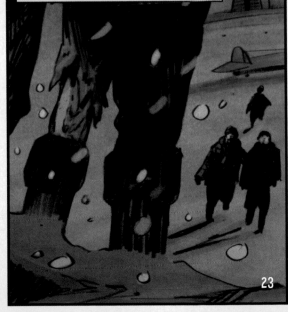

The two women had a difficult trek back to their camp, but they made it safely. It took two months for Nina to recover from her injuries. But once healed, she went straight back to flying with the squadron.

23

25

VICTORY

Despite the Soviets' best efforts, the Germans kept winning battle after battle. They advanced deep into Soviet territory.

They're burning all of our crops. Our beautiful country is burning.

They're moving so fast. How can we stop them?

In 1943 the turning point came. The Soviet army stopped the Germans at the Battle of Stalingrad, the largest battle of the war. More than 2 million Soviet and German soldiers were killed, wounded, or captured. Soviet forces defeated Germany at Stalingrad and began to push the Germans back.

The women's squadrons followed the fighting on the ground. They moved forward each time Soviet soldiers took back land from the Nazis.

As the Soviet troops advanced, the women's missions became more difficult.

Soviet and German troops were soon fighting so close together that the pilots could not tell one side from the other.

One morning, the Night Witches were sleeping in their tents after flying all night. They heard soldiers outside. But they didn't know if the men were Soviet or German troops. They prepared to fight.

CLUNK
CLUNK
CLATTER

Shhhh. Don't let them know we're here.

Just in time, they realized the soldiers were on their side.

We've been fighting all night to push the Germans back. You won't have to worry about their antiaircraft guns anymore.

That's good news! Perhaps this hateful war will be over soon. Then we can go home.

HEROES OF THE MOTHERLAND

June 24, 1945. It was over. Nazi Germany was defeated. More than 40,000 Soviet soldiers marched through Moscow's Red Square in a great parade to celebrate the end of the war.

Members of the 46th Night Bomber Regiment took part in the parade. Many wore the Hero of the Soviet Union medal, the highest honor anyone in the Soviet military could receive.

Some men in the Soviet air force knew how skilled the female pilots were. The women had flown hundreds of missions in old airplanes and survived many dangers.

The commander of the Night Bomber Regiment recommended two of the best young female pilots to join the air force academy. He believed that they should stay in the military. Maybe they would become test pilots, or even command their own squadrons.

But when the women arrived, the general of the academy called them to his office.

You are heroes of our Motherland. You showed what women can do when their help is needed.

But studying in the academy is hard work. You lost so much strength during the war, we must protect your health.

The pilots understood that the general was rejecting them.

Other women who served in the squadrons wanted to be finished with war. They hoped to return to their families and help rebuild their country.

Years later, pilot Nadia Popova said, *"Peace was the only thing we cared about. We just wanted to return to a normal life."*

Nadia had flown more than 850 missions during the war. Like all of the women she served with, Nadia was proud of the part she played in freeing her homeland.

Nadia earned several awards for her service, including Hero of the Soviet Union, the Order of Lenin, and the Order of the Red Banner. After the war, she worked as a flight instructor.

Later in life, Nadia remembered her time as one of the Night Witches. *"I can still imagine myself as a young girl, up there in my little bomber. And I ask myself, 'Nadia, how did you do it?'"*

29

GLOSSARY

academy (uh-KAD-uh-mee)—a school that teaches special subjects, such as skills needed to become an officer in the military

bail out (BAYL OUT)—to jump out of an airplane and parachute to safety

canvas (KAN-vuhs)—a type of strong, heavy cloth usually used to make tents and ship sails

cockpit (KOK-pit)—the area in an airplane where the pilot and navigator sit

comrade (KOM-rad)—a good friend, or someone you fight with in battle; people in the Soviet Union often called each other "comrade" to show that they were all working together for their country

front line (FRUHNT LYN)—the area nearest an enemy's position during a war

Nazi Germany (NOT-see JER-muh-nee)—a period of time from 1933 to 1945 when Germany was controlled by the Nazi Party and led by Adolph Hitler

Soviet Union (SOH-vee-et YOON-yuhn)—a former group of 15 republics that included Russia, Ukraine, and other nations of eastern Europe and northern Asia

squadron (SKWAHD-ruhn)—a military unit, often a group of military pilots and aircraft

stall (STAHL)—when a vehicle's engine suddenly stops running

READ MORE

Dell, Pamela. *The Soviet Night Witches: Brave Women Bomber Pilots of World War II*. Women and War. North Mankato, MN: Capstone Press, 2018.

Owens, Lisa L. *Women Pilots of World War II*. Heroes of World War II. Minneapolis: Lerner Publications, 2018.

Simons, Lisa M Bolt. *The U.S. WASP: Trailblazing Women Pilots of World War II*. Women and War. North Mankato, MN: Capstone Press, 2018.

CRITICAL THINKING QUESTIONS

- Some of the pilots who flew in the women's squadrons were only 17 years old. Imagine that you were one of these young women. Why would you leave your family and school to join an air force squadron and face terrible dangers?

- More than 26 million people in the Soviet Union died during World War II. Imagine if that many Americans had died in the war. What effect do you think that would have had on U.S. citizens? How would people in the United States remember the war today?

- The Night Witches showed great bravery during the war. But some male officers still opposed having women pilots in the air force. Why do you think they felt this way?

INTERNET SITES

Fearless Female Russion Pilots
https://www.dailymail.co.uk/news/article-4706856/Female-Soviet-pilots-transformed-colourised-WWII-photos.html

Meet the Night Witches
https://www.history.com/news/meet-the-night-witches-the-daring-female-pilots-who-bombed-nazis-by-night

The Night Witches
http://elinorflorence.com/blog/night-witches

INDEX